Simon's Cat

Simon's Cat

IT'S A DOG'S LIFE

CANONGATE

Simon Tofield

First published in Great Britain, the USA and Canada in 2019
by Canongate Books Ltd, 14 High Street, Edinburgh EH1 1TE

Distributed in the USA by Publishers Group West and in Canada by Publishers Group Canada

canongate.co.uk

1

British Library Cataloguing-in-Publication Data
A catalogue record for this book is available on
request from the British Library

ISBN 978 1 78689 700 8

Printed and bound in China by 1010 Printing International Ltd

For Zoë and James

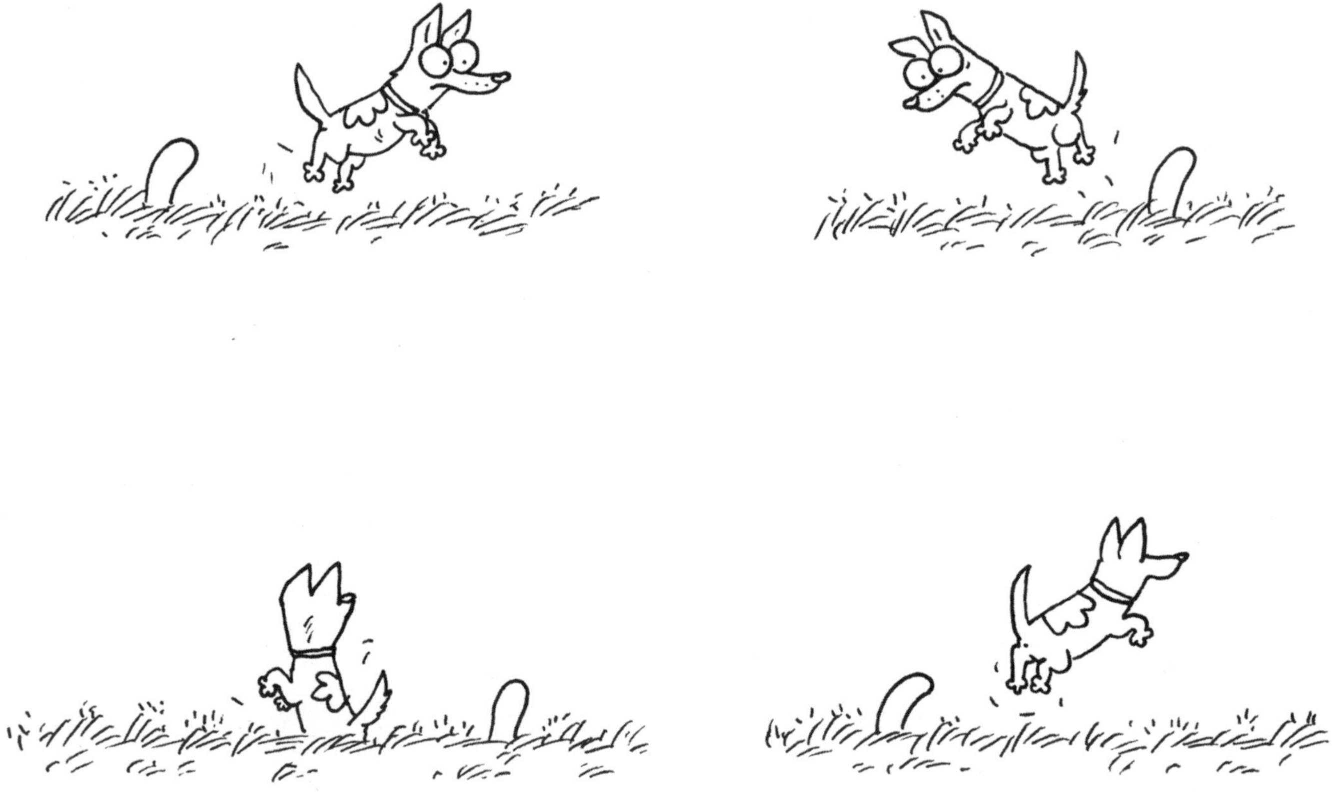

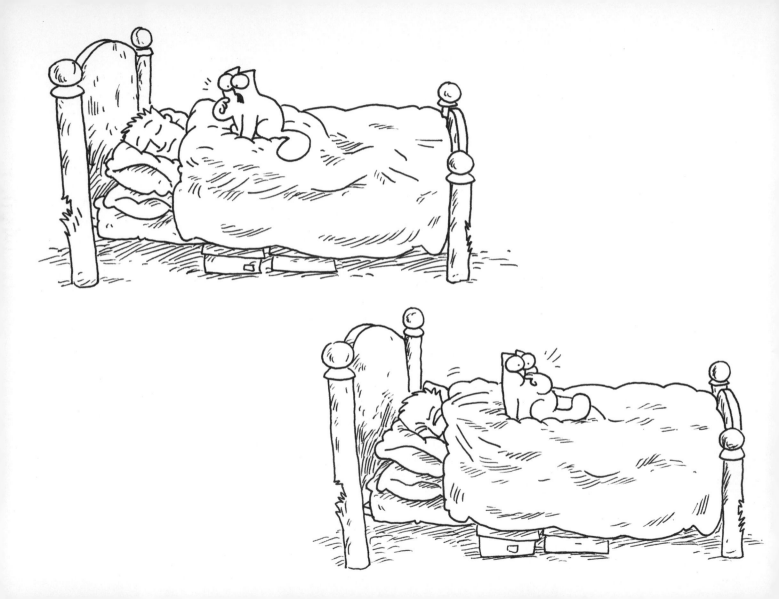

Acknowledgements

Thanks to Zoë and James Tofield, Emma Randell, Theresa Ward, Edwin Eckford, Liza Nechaeva, Georgi Chapman, Rachel Thorn, Alice Bernardi, Jane Smith, Hannah Knowles and all the Canongate Team.

For all your Simon's Cat goodies, check out the webshop
at simonscat.com